HARROWIN

Also by Cecily Nicholson

From the Poplars
Triage
Wayside Sang

All published by Talonbooks

HARROWINGS

POEMS

CECILY NICHOLSON

TALONBOOKS

Talonbooks
9259 Shaughnessy Street, Vancouver, British Columbia, Canada V6P 6R4
talonbooks.com

Talonbooks is located on xʷməθkʷəy̓əm, Sḵwx̱wú7mesh, and səl̓ilwətaʔɬ Lands.

First printing: 2022

Typeset in Avenir
Printed and bound in Canada on 100% post-consumer recycled paper

Cover and interior design by Typesmith
Cover image by Jan Wade

Talonbooks acknowledges the financial support of the Canada Council for the Arts, the Government of Canada through the Canada Book Fund, and the Province of British Columbia through the British Columbia Arts Council and the Book Publishing Tax Credit.

Canadä |●| Canada Council   Conseil des arts   BRITISH   BRITISH COLUMBIA
              for the Arts   du Canada   COLUMBIA   ARTS COUNCIL
                                                                  An agency of the Province of British Columbia

Library and Archives Canada Cataloguing in Publication

Title: Harrowings : poems / by Cecily Nicholson.
Names: Nicholson, Cecily, author.
Description: Includes bibliographical references.
Identifiers: Canadiana 20220210004 | ISBN 9781772014051 (softcover)
Classification: LCC PS8627.I2393 H37 2022 | DDC c811/.6—dc23

for my brother Daniel B. playing live at the stampede
and love to Caroline G., wherever you are

carver (a hand in relief)

place is my hand on the relief cast of Carver's
       the cast is cool

hand vibrates to feel the whole surface at once
memory an indent sense of prints

extent charged
tips through index and middle metacarpals

     it was a passing shadow of a bird

at rest
   my hand settling on Hathaway's sculpture

associatory, simple elements

the store of atmosphere, pounds of water
                    brought as property

            to situate within genealogy
giving backs to land an intellectual and art history

idle moments put
                    to gathering
        to care
                    to share food

to not solely succumb to logics of land/crop/harvest
as required by institutions of slavery and capital

*the country ... wears a rich and luxuriant aspect**

---

* Frederick Douglass, "First of August Celebration at Dawn Settlement, Canada West –
Public Meeting at Chatham – Visit to the Elgin Settlement at Buxton," *Frederick
Douglass' Paper* (August 11, 1854), 2.

In 1854 Frederick Douglass set out from Rochester, New York, to attend a gathering, to mark the twenty-year anniversary of the "West India Emancipation," the First of August Celebration at the Dawn Settlement for fugitive slaves – travelling most of the three-hundred-mile journey by rail "except sixteen miles between Chatham and the Settlement referred to"* by wagon. Douglass journeyed through the Traditional Territories of the Haudenosaunee, Mississauga, Attawandaron, Anishinaabe ⊲ᓂᏕᐃᐧᐃV, and Myaamia Nations to arrive in the "historic" county of "Kent."

About that 1854 journey Douglass remarks: "In regard to the place, itself, it is one of the most beautiful and desirable localities for agriculture, commerce and education, which we know of in Canada West."† I reflect further on fugitivity of that time, and upon life in the near aftermath of slavery as the dominion of canada formed. The language and logics of farm stem from structures of settler colonialism even if they embody emancipatory practices. This makes for complicated dreams.

---

* Douglass, "First of August Celebration," 2.

† Ibid.

*sufficiently free from the fatigue of this journey**

rounding a corner to *The Song of the Lark*
the light so familiar I had to sit

for many voices, starts
a moth alit, a rhetorical Du Bois

faltering inches of progress the dawning
as the sundial says to the soil

                                        your auntie up the road just now recalls

---

*   Douglass, "First of August Celebration," 2.

to drop quietly in what may be considered

*no velvet road**

sun slow reaches by wagon over
tracts
      the soil losing time and time again to corn

history as decomposition

tillage machinery entangles the surface
aerobic stems with roots in microflora

field against nature – natural anchored in rot

pasturage planting regeneration plots to pick rocks
in tandem with machines

my first job was walking in formation, a child field hand
alert to small rocks frost-heaved to the surface

---

*   Douglass, "First of August Celebration," 2.

uncompetitive roots with varied depths
of soil nutrients under restorative cover

leafy tansy resists the eager
and unproductive

seedling thugs invasive and exotic
sweet-smelling dandelion, its yellow

a butterfly in milkweed
burdock tea keeps meaning to steep

ovum leaves from our youthful brambles

clover, mustard, and winter rye flowering tells

sun, the morning hours till the soil clung to grasses
sweet switch and june

cultivated squares, the runoff
slide of swill ditches

order around holds the farmstead stamps
in a bird's eyes

willow – acacia of the endless plains
in some act of literature – my lion and tiger, my august

morning all hours wound; all hours are the same

behind the barn, across the treeline and a ditch
distinguishing property

out cornrows along thin strips of habitat

patched and neutral
hand-me-downs

pry apart fence wires to go between

tilting gusts
                        thin riparian trunks

by a near-dry creek
folds a cabin collapsed and cellarless on the ground

*Soft purl the streams, the birds renew their
notes**

tempers dim
breathing through the nose, shoulders bare
                        cooling

back amid a chorus of whirrs, grasses shake and curl

sweet and pounceable body

I can feel my place in extraction
hear how to centre / how hard to decentre

            discourse that's found me
            determining

in an arrival of dark evening stars Venus
casts shadows on the dark firmament

---

*   Phillis Wheatley, "A Hymn to the Evening" (1773), *The Collected Works of Phillis
    Wheatley*, 58.

... know something more in detail about such subjects as the following:

a) *The constituents of plants.*

b) *The materials which furnish plant food.*

c) *The condition these materials must be in before the plant can use them.*

d) *The constituents of soils.*

e) *What forms and quantities of plant food to use on different soils and crops.**

---

*   George W. Carver, *How to Build Up and Maintain the Virgin Fertility of Our Soils* (1936), 3.

well black on the nether side, it will rain

use the hours, don't count them

one for the rook, one for the crow
one to die, and one to grow

it's later than you think

Well: it is barely spring. Winter lingered
this year we need to dig a new well.
Knowing enough of septic tanks
and cisterns, something of metal alloys
comprising pipes and the insulation
prayer that keeps things from bursting
on the coldest snowbelt nights many
were awake but for different reasons.
Hearing creaks, know enough to be wary.

Early lessons in infrastructure I absolve
myself of worry in this future as a renter
in a cloud, tethered to networks and systems
city miles up from rain barrels and arable.

To plan a well could use a diviner in advance
there was something to do and somewhere to
start when the pond did not indicate potable.
Fallow soil sprouts rocks and thugs and was
out of the way so that happened to be where
the diviner encouraged a backhoe to dig. There
every foot deeper cost more money.

Adults went to work, and children
went to school a whole day returns
to no new source. Pinched faces at
the window murmur about what will
happen should they have to stop.
Maybe there's insufficient water on
this property, and likely more debt.

In the garden, just above the staked tomato plants, a hand peeks into view. The fingers and thumb are stained grey green past the first knuckle with tomato tar and dusted lightly with yellow pollen. The thumb and forefinger gently hold up two vibrant tomato blossoms, green sepals and stems covered in shimmering white tangles of fuzz. In one flower, the stamen is just about to open, and in the other, the stamen is unfurling and uncurling.*

---

*   Cecily Nicholson and Mercedes Eng, "Restorative Practices" (2021), *BlackFlash*, image description of *Tomato Blood*.

somatically, my body remembers "farm" as a rurally entrenched kid
as I lived once cultivated and punctuated

by the occasional bush and ditches that weren't much at all
like these rolling hills songed in mission bells

in reach of cemetery lawns across the road away
                                        that *feel* familiar – now   .

field as a playground – ward youth intermittently involved
in state care that cared less –
       I care more, and for more about and around me

la paperson observes that we cannot reckon with

"… how Black people are often confronted
by the *impossibility* of settlement,

     because antiblackness
   positions Black people as 'out of place' on land."*

     adrift – a current, the harrowing undulatory

deft carves in smooth turns handle
   a moment or two of river

        where have I been a settler is where I am
restored   returning to efforts of cultivation

---

*   la paperson, "Settler Colonialism Is a Set of Technologies," in *A Third University Is Possible* (2017).

I think on Vicky Mochama's discussion* of mutual aid and other
reminders

that these practices are not new, rather, long-standing traditions
                    instilled in Black community and experience

after-carceral
end of days stitch together the sewn and sung drums reconstructed

---

*   Vicky Mochama, "Black Communities Have Known about Mutual Aid All Along,"
     Walrus (September 1, 2020).

reminded, as Toronto Black Farmers note, that communities will thrive "when the people are nourished, when they are educated, and when they come together as a community: food is the nexus between them."[*]

reconstituted, I consider Paul Taylor's organizing on food insecurity.[†] problems that cannot be answered with "casseroles made in community kitchens …"

reconnected given networked roots like Soul Fire Farm, feeding community, honouring relatives, seeding sovereignty, farming practices, as "each one teach one"[‡]

* Toronto Black Farmers, "About Us" (website).

† Jennifer Foden, "What Is Food Insecurity? FoodShare's Paul Taylor Explains (Plus What Canadians Can Do about It)," Food Network (June 25, 2020).

‡ Soul Fire Farm, "Each One, Teach One" (website).

to practise

      given the service of labours
          herein my reallocated labour

          (passages via free gardens)

to honour

fish pepper plants made way to Chesepiooc table settings
Horace Pippin, a painter, gave seeds to H. Ralph Weaver, a beekeeper

A shallow grey ceramic bowl with crackled glaze rests on a wooden table. Light from a window pours in, creating bright spots on the glaze. Within the bowl, an assortment of chili peppers in a range of sizes and a rainbow of colours. Some are solid, while others are striped or tinted with a gradient, one colour at the tip, melting into another colour as it moves up to the stem: pale yellow, green and yellow, green and red, deep purple, orange, lilac, and red. Leaning at the front of the bowl is a list of the pepper types handwritten on lined paper in thick, black marker: "Fish, Black Hungarian, Buena Mulata, Hinklehatz, Sugar Rush Peach, Carolina Reaper."*

---

*   Nicholson and Eng, "Restorative Practices," image description of *Peppers*.

simmering young pale peppers translucent
coveted cream sauce for fish
        hence the name

the first time
        shimmery and feminine

heat is a subjective test

        one for sensitive
one is prickly, once flaring at the hip

all in all, a farm is a good teacher

farming out from under the heat
abiding in trenches

       hierarchies of settlement
       bodies positioned
       property divisions

sovereignty confronted in occupying and murderous ways

honeybees, pigs outside pens
vegetables fenced in loam

turned casings

scrape of sprays
the height of Scovilles sear the eyes

law-enforcement grades
the indecent haste of colony

returning to labour for seed migration
and husbandry is to farm is

to food that you contribute
to attend and cultivate

stall pen bed coop pasture and cage

relations
in an effort of preservation

manual labour
pressure-canned fish and candied jalapeños

light render and pollination, I sleep
ill enough
                too long
                or dreaming half woke

an array maturing green to red
the hottest
            though orange even

virginal to soiled
streaked bloody midsection tangles

at the measure

    the presence of twilight
fertility and life I could never hold in me

    springs from thumbs

a perfectly verdant ancestry

            partially illuminated
       sky so civil, nautical, and astronomical

carceral and climate do not pull apart in justice

is a view of the coast across the narrowest reach

all the water inside movings in tides
like the sea

an ebb bulges high

our bare soles warm the soil at planting times

a ~~voice that will~~ clamour: correspondences 1-4

for community at Emma's Acres

Engaging in restorative justice, holding a free, aspiring organic,
and no-till green space, Emma's Acres provides food for
families of incarcerated people and low-income families living
in the food-insecure city of Mission, in an area currently known
as the Fraser Valley, in the Pacific Northwest.
These last few years volunteering with a farm led by
people who were formerly incarcerated, I've engaged in
correspondence, sometimes poetic, with community inside.

for a rattling mind and cooped-up body
ecliptic this apparent path

    the best time to plant
from cultivated and ponded poetics

four clefs incline
in mutual will-o'-the-wisps
    and noise tremors

lift 19″ TVs and manual typewriters
soil and irrigation, the infrastructure rows

correspondence 1: The collage's top half is within a greenhouse. A well-worn, wood-framed whiteboard hangs against a dusty, semi-opaque, raindrop-splattered window. The whiteboard is filled with black marker mapping out the crops within two greenhouses. "Greenhouse #2!," on the left, has a modest number of long rows, a soil-sifting area, and a note to "Keep it clean, kids!" with hearts dotting each letter *i*. "Greenhouse No. #1! 2019," on the right, has two rows of fifteen tables each marked out, mostly growing greens. Planting dates are listed. The bottom half of the collage, the greenhouse whiteboard floating over it, is a close-up of a lightly rippling lake with sparse, puffy clouds and a mountain peak reflected. Only hints of shape and colour are visible beneath the water's murky surface.*

---

* Nicholson, "correspondence 1," ~~a voice that will~~ clamour (*The Pandemic Is a Portal*, SFU Galleries, 2020), image description.

fell into the mud slipping in clay a bed makes its rise
yellowing rot along the row and mire

in the house with no dog the straw gets taken up
and new plants are growing all the time

ginger can't grow without seeming to dance

beneath a lone plantain far from home I cling
for a moment, then turn back to hauling

select measures of phosphate hues and potassium

heavily fertilized carrots all hopped up with hairy limbs
line the coop, early to pickle

these babes woke in wild nitrogen dreams

                                        the light in here

I should stay in this greenhouse all the time

the light is the third lake you had to run early morning
save quartering all afternoon

or risk a catch of storm

this year *I will* … remember and make a habit of watering
the lettuce and Detroit Special beets that run the balcony

a magnificent row witnessed and admired
on a hotbed as sprouts

it's that kind of light in here

                                        here to you
                                   from here, to you

Rock piles: how my brother and I, the youngest,
imagine stories in and of the dirt as it descends,
which bones and artifacts will become present,
the butterfly stone fossils became possessions.
Which culture we were supposed to make fun of
ourselves, the dirty fingers brown and browner
overturn new rocks in the rock pile. Freer from
restraint the mindsets of diggers on our common

Hunting in rock piles the light stretched longer
enough to risk our feet catching crags of dark
matter. We formed adjacent rock beds; beds made
of rocks, we set ourselves in to watch the sundown
over and over the same fields. The sky cast bush
shadows an acre off relief in a thin band of horizon
stars rose brightly and never set, circling the best days

aglow filled our hearts
as if our homeland
hometown.

Well, and finally, after winter nights' paved roads
whitened completely as flakes piled up past cladding
and through ditches.

The snow fence bending
one ruddy weak slat after another against the draft
whose very purpose seemed to penetrate. The fences
figure again and again. For now, iron rods in constant
burrows of rust-chronicling weather.

Winter such as this pushed deeper into spring
flattening buds and their longing burst of fragrance.
A relief, the time between bird calls lessening. Relief
when finally, the smell of mud struck consciousness,
like lilacs only sweeter. As the heat of the sun registered
warmth on skin, trickles of water coursed the driveway
rutting to a lower ditch as the water table began to rise.

it is hard to write from inside   a brick house

easier to remember infrastructure
hinge and joinery

welds and glue, horsehair plaster
storied layers and layers of paint and wallpaper

office extensions
barely aware of the arrival of news

radio-thin waves the flapping clothesline
haunts

how hard it is to write from inside

I look up from that outside spot to site the angles of eaves
troughs and drainage

pretending it was my sandbox and my swing
my acidic cherry tree, the lenticels in bark

reddish-brown undertows
        closest family to family I've never outgrown

in the belly
how much easier it is to write my hands grasping at soil

Vegetable Seeds › Beet Seeds › Detroit Supreme Beet Seeds

long-time standard green
     with a maroon tinge

           full sun or partial shade

seeds begun in a cold and damp state
their living enzymes turn

eyes to the sun
making the most of time

shipped in envelopes
heirlooms

land with a wealth of seeds

able to build and strengthen soil
hold these babes in the palm of your hand

    and return in practice

sacks of cash crop dominance

the ravine may have been arable but not navigable
everywhere else …

what lies beneath the pavement for miles
surrounding the tallest buildings
corporate

prime arable   deep

the sun endures, rivers remedy

Deshkaan-ziibi, about thirty miles from Waawiyaataan
and sixty miles out of Detroit

The pro-slavery party of the United States is the aggressive party on this continent. It is the serpent that aims to swallow all others. It is meet then to make strongholds, and, if need be, defend them; that will be the most effective check to greediness of land and negroes.*

*   Mary A. Shadd, *A Plea for Emigration, or Notes of Canada West, in Its Moral, Social, and Political Aspect: With Suggestions respecting Mexico, W. Indies and Vancouver's Island, for the Information of Colored Emigrants* (1852), 42.

narrative deep ruts the DNA sweeps
into the quickening dusk

an essential community outside

inside multiculturalism the big mouths,
bellies, and bottom lines celebrate with food

seasonal *presente*

all strength to traverse the dark rural roads

prime dairy is powder

prime meat
hamburger fed on tiring pastures

this is butcher paper
this is a freezer of animal protein
and a patrinormative sinking of teeth

burger wrapper catches the wind
                    and drifts its miles

to rest in a furrow about the garden acre

*But how do you grow a poet?**

phrases the cadence hums inside the city
each plant potted and given away

in iteration

dying on the sole windowsill of your quarters
                    I'll bring you another

speaking with trees
reassemble

        unsee the wringing

unhitch the trailer, leave it there to gather invaders
its hardened wheels will sink into ruts

---

*   Robert Kroetsch, *Seed Catalogue* (1977), 15.

listen … years of food service, labour
                    lost and found kitchens

listen … langar feeding people

in line a kind efficient
rice, dal, sabzi, chana, roti, kheer, sheera

balance, scraps of consciousness
beyond a racial parochialism

responsibility to people who you do not know
ways to be on land

And I've been waiting long
*For an earth song.**

kisan-mazdoor ekta zindabad

justicia migrante

food for spirit

song

---

* Langston Hughes, "Earth Song" (1925), in *Black Nature: Four Centuries of African American Nature Poetry*, 342.

networks in the motion of till

a measure of memory

wind blew the trunks twisted
ice-scoured basins

a mesh of roots makes slow haste

in the motion of till
towards the bluff of an old shoreline

Rise of pond: after the migration stop was drained and we fought and lost again to the chemical pond lined with black tarp, we turned to the front-yard swamp. To bend to pond the green life that fought to hold the other to an emulsion state neither water nor mud, somewhat tadpoles. Where catching frogs was possible, and even still today one can realize terror in another creature being trapped and held.

Holding up a frog by its two back legs an instant over so fast few will witness it like the ruddy farmer boy who – died before my age now having heartened out winter after hard winter – driving by in a tractor, broke into laughter. We could not hear it, but it was nice to imagine. And it was the frogs, not us, who made it clowning, this holding-a-frog-by-its-two-back-legs dance. Underbrush running to trees.

Stump of stumps: stump of course used to be tree
though we remember it best as a stage or seating
we sat upon it at the end of the driveway watching
a perfectly red sunset. And we knew about sailors
and we knew we had relations on islands who shipped
and were shipped, and we knew what it would mean
to be sailors. To master a sextant of tabulations.

We had excursions, twice, on great lakes as servants on sailboats.
We took commands out the lean, thin mouth of uncles and strangers.
We ran to the prow and we ran to the stern, and we were not sickened.

Holding our breath, we learned how to float in fresh water.
We were able to swim, our bellies could buoy us, our breath
brethren-deep, each intake boosting our bobbing corporal
to the surface. Dimension-deep in music poetry edged a farm.

When stump was still a tree a suitor on exchange from Italy
sat to strum his guitar underneath. Having walked a country
block and a half from his host family's home to sit there making
songs in Spanish, the language of love he later told me, was
a good place to rest. They – someone or other called him –
as only a queer query made sense to my fifteen years ugly.
Only our queer efforts could make this music. We held the line.

The tree was an early stage. I wish I knew more about it.
I thought a maple. Or some hardwood grey-eyed and all
the grey eyes since. Those efforts to take a stand, the
many last stands of trees along a field of cultivated tracts.
To venture down those roads, to travel in a pack or alone.

pouring rain an afternoon early fall
left the lake of the q̓íc̓əy̓ under police escort

the police had waved hello rocking the canoe with turbulence

powerboats running at us for hours
        had rumbled by our quiet camp every evening

the lake over stern draws
agitation welds

                worth what power concedes

        for four nights with shore as the lake leaves and returns
                speaking of sturgeon

to witness ospreys
the dry mouth of the streambed, physical confines for future water

cares

the weather

                                        what is o'clock

watching animals ready
        for weather

hewn   primeval

                        listening to trees

trees meet their reflection at the water's edge

anticipate my heartbeat

this rake of fir sizing up the foothills
a jutting lay in the rain shadow

matches effortlessly

the seed stayed within its cell
bursting container within containers

beds of germinating sprouts bloom love
exploding the limits of hothouse

correspondence 2: An ultra close-up of weathered chicken-wire fence in the foreground. At the centre is one hexagon of wire built by the junction of four lengths of wire and the twists created as each wire passes the other to travel its journey to the next junction. Behind the fence, the image is blurred: a large hen house, one bag of feed resting against the exterior wall, and a solitary hen pecking at the dirt just outside the entry. The hen house is a fading fire-engine red with a white gable, visually playing with the white hen and her red comb and wattle.*

---

* Nicholson, "correspondence 2," ~~a voice that will~~ clamour, image description.

everything comes in so fast seedlings set to row
the weeds between the water burst
with curlicue intelligence
                    my hair has this tendency

the strawberries lushed up tall been less a month
they grew four times the height

ready in the coming weeks
tried a few pink ones, sweet, even now enough

weed companions, mostly good company
though we tackle the endless bramble

flowing in from the .ditch
the brimming farm

all the fields work to yield
all the fields are worked

I can see a pulse in the lettuce
whorls of storms about plants and skies

Georgina's garden remembers itself
years ahead practical for the tobacco

wasps paper the totem base
and the hail pierces leaves of wailing

trill the birds about
goldfinch faerie clouds glint in small gestures

turkey vultures tried to set up
they took four, two hens left mangled behind

now this new netting flickers
its new-car-lot streamers in metallic flash

birds of prey circle but fear the landing

Memoirs are always too soon
and perhaps that means never.

A nail that stuck out of a broom
to the head that was punctured.

Scarring: from that time the dog at the babysitter's farm took my head in its mouth.

Having had four dogs at any time and not one ever having taken mine or anyone's head in its mouth this was a time to remain calm.

Once one had nibbled too hard hungry enough to bite and fingers of children being so brittle. Worried for that dog.

The dog bed that was a comfort of fleas and poets fallen and hidden, a kind of comfort worth visiting.

I have little memory of it, just two faint marks on either cheek.

There were other dogs, and someone had to carry a crowbar
      past certain properties the dogs come running.

There are farmers armed
shots warn from a hill, the downward trajectories unaccounted for

      there was skin petted. There were wrists held.
    There were weapons hoisted. There were beatings.

There, backed into a corner clinking the pretty coloured bottles lining
a low kitchen windowsill. Dust, a slanting roof.

The organized running, learning to run.
These gravel-road-knees sets of scars.
Trying hand signals that we were taught
in gym class. Like the farmer on a tractor
was watching to see which direction
I would turn a quarter mile back. Still,
I grew twice as fast on my red BMX
from the tire company. I had saved for it.

First, I saved for a clock radio that raised me
for the earlier, short bus, and summer work
to pay some bills. Cycling my early commute
red was wheels, the frame, spokes, and a seat.
To be like the sister who had gotten on a bike
and just rode it, skipping past training wheels.
To be legendary among boys for having skills.

Labours cracked along the bridge. I trust nose scars.
I trust we have something in common. Even if it was
from years of playing hockey, backhand, broad beam,
that chainsaw or tire shrapnel or an obscene breakout,
chances are we have some things common between us.

This iron rod purposed itself a fence pole, always prodded up from the banks of winter. And it had no intent. Triumphant that day I got taken to the hospital. The golf-ball lump pushed my skin permanently into a subtle crease that matches my frown even now. I think it works. The doctor, kind, leaning in talking directly to me, changed something.

hover

       a collection of places where most days there are harvests
most days hinge ready to creak

we show our best simple mechanic bodies leveraged to adapt

parents would not become grand
               kept to one side of a border or another

eventually they fell away
                            sympathetic nervous
child come through this sliding-glass moment to wicket down a cue

bus-charted highways for the city now, more than rural relations

country
        heads marked in rain shadows of trauma restore
                              with poured joinery
shared histories of repair form new classroom

ditches, virtuosity seams property rivering the melt
as earthquakes loosen lakes

        trenches lined in landscape fabric
            rustle my silt further and further inland

"Grace" boys about the mall called to me, back when
        I could not reply to "What's your name?"

        twine opening corridors of scalp to town
sun feels differently set differently through skyline teeth

a thin yield of cabbages speckled in rot everywhere
blight excels as a matter of course

a few barrows heavy still farming enough to truck
for piecemeal wages, the long rows repeat sundown

thatched hats lift to the breeze, seasonal conditions
remitting home, occupancy, groceries

set foot on a plane for the first time at twenty-two
spring before my first wedding lasted a while longer

a culvert blend, a Malecón flair, versions of summery

form of scales, needles, feathers, or fans*

fall returns my back to sit against a fence post, eye level
with a few missed scrags of wheat given chance to rot

to wonder the life of the field that will or was cast before

winter comes and goes renting quiet evenings

the dirt hardened by dew simply frozen, our adjacent airs
on relatively calm nights are *intime* holds radiating
                                      vapours to lift and vanish

kin fictions enter and leave systems bioluminescence
stormwater runoff the edge of a farm unmooring berths

---

*   Marshall Shepard, "Frozen Dew, Frost, and Freezes – Do You Know the Difference?,"
    Forbes (November 3, 2019).

correspondence 3: The field has been left to wild in this collage. The top third is an upside-down landscape with rolling hills in the background, then a stand of evergreen trees, and the foreground is green space on the farm, greenhouses and various small wooden buildings. The buildings are framed by one dark carved pole, and the base of another, made of pale wood. Grass and flowering weeds have been left to flourish. The centre third is filled with darkening rain clouds. At the bottom, a close-up of rows of beets, shot with the camera on the ground, focusing on the rich red stems and veiny green leaves of the beet tops. Filling the space between rows, grasses and weeds reach for life, already half as tall as the crops. Beyond the beets, the evergreen trees and long greenhouse from the top image can be seen, but no longer upside down.*

---

* Nicholson, "correspondence 3," ~~a voice that will~~ *clamour*, image description.

bass wraps around us we have not met

folks been gathering this Pen Pack material costs may this

what electronic equipment would you like (see personal effects list)?
only if available. no Wi-Fi or Bluetooth items

in a list I'd wish you to it

gone solitary moments undesired

could this

electronic 19" TV (720p HD LED TV / highest temporal resolution possible)
with some feet of coaxial cable to situate anywhere a room, *allow it*

may improve be approved to connect outside
to play Nintendo (up to 10 games)

may you get to listen to a stereo, to a Discman (CD player),
with headphones

for all a 4-outlet power bar PS One (up to 10 games)

for the people
need the air to move, with one 5.5" plastic fan

rechargeable batteries and a battery charger for the people

reading lamp with 2 extra light bulbs, please (when I read this I cried)

reading lamp light, the typewriter is manual and electric – what will it say?

an alarm clock newest of new items, may you have some new things under

one or more of the following personal identifiers:
   a) a serial number
   b) inmate name
   c) an engraved locator number
   d) a barcode

Let our emigrants so abolitionize and strengthen neighboring positions as to promote the prosperity and harmony of the whole.*

---

*   Shadd, *A Plea for Emigration*, 42.

*even their bare hands**

carrying water
carrying hay

to lift rocks
pick rocks

heft a bucket
shovel dirt
shovel manure and wood chips

hoist an implement, balance a basket

carry each other
we *get to* carry each other

---

*   Peggy Bristow, "'Whatever You Raise in the Ground You Can Sell It in Chatham': Black Women in Buxton and Chatham, 1850-65," in *"We're Rooted Here and They Can't Pull Us Up": Essays in African Canadian Women's History* (1994), 88.

help for the hard times

arms reach towards the camera

                                 palms turned up

cupping pastel chicken eggs:

        pink, green, orange, and speckled orange

the eggs are fresh from the henhouse,
smudges of shit across the shells.

the person stands on a spot covered with straw

cleared and worked the land, planted, harvested, shared and sold
crops and fed families, they also made time to plant and enjoy flowers*

outskirts, a glossary of oddities
particles released from a comet

the calendar in tides with time corrections

owning tools and draft animals

home remedies farming for good
take what is needed

each careworn path lifting and carrying

---

*   Daniel G. Hill, *The Freedom-Seekers: Blacks in Early Canada* (1992), 80.

a glade in isolation, sound carries after a tide keeps turning
shout out Chloe Ngakosso
                              to find a voice

"We see you, we are sorry and we are sad."

And there are consequences.

and the hours keep turning, each day begins a morning
mosses, ferns, horsetails, the canopy widens

                    To shield your poet from the burning day*

*   Phillis Wheatley, "A Hymn to the Morning" (1773), *The Collected Works of Phillis Wheatley*, 56.

If thirteen then barely, maybe it was late summer.
In a little, pink, mesh top, and sunglasses and cut-offs
bronzed – right lateral recumbent, inciting rebellion.
My left-arm angles, my head propped purpose labours
the combed-back hair pour-some-sugar-on-me prowl
assembled on the lawn. Kitty corner, country block over.

On that family's front lawn while they were gone
to work in fields and always out back during summer
my friend and I posed side to soil our midriffs
lay on exhausted sod incapable of crop.
the hard, dry surface of uneven lawn, its underbelly
mesh of shallow roots on the graft. Nobody drove by

home,

it's stone sills on the sunny side warming
slowly as a motor in the distance strums closer

tummy aches of exhaust and oatmeal

the birds scatter in murmurs dipping over
the morning

a collective investigation of a black walnut
and what makes it black stains yellow

facing southerly winds
facing wells, and hills, and prospects

correspondence 4: The top two-thirds are an ultra close-up of a red lettuce leaf, taken from beneath. The leaf is dew-dropped, and sunlight penetrates the green segments, but not the red. The leaf is wide and ruffled, and it's positioned as if it's an awning protecting the camera from the sun for the second picture in the collage. The second picture, layered beneath the red lettuce, is a blurry, wider shot of many rows of varieties of lettuce, round and full, at their prime for harvest. Between the rows, vibrant green ground cover. A lone figure wearing a hat stands amid the rows, gazing out across the field.*

---

* Nicholson, "correspondence 4," ~~a voice that will~~ *clamour*, image description.

counter, transpose

been these few quiet aches in the key bone
of the shoulder girdle serving to link
the scapula and sternum
on the same stave transpose
collarbone

as the heirloom tomatoes gone wild

the leaders strung up; new leaders woven in
leaders taking away from the plant lopped off

in the big beef corner of the market
tomatoes pulling ten feet topple the structures

yeah, I'm bent at the hips. the slipping back
the rural youth in skill-less joyless grinds

I remember. but this is my reallocated labour
my mutual aid, my gratitude given the respite

the fresh takes on abolition
the best insight into agricultural complexes

my gratitude resting, rested reading
bathing, swimming, running … earned

include the number of hours working for wages
working overtime alone or in partnership

working directly towards the operation of a farm
with/out formal pay arrangements
(e.g., assisting in seeding, doing accounts)

include indentured geopolitics, include incarcerated labours

to hold a blistering Carolina Reaper in repose is the drive

it is the roads getting narrower, more murmurs of blackbirds
two eagles a branch not minding us

roadside purchases, pick-your-own pacing years counting beans

those seedlings six now eight feet a witness to irrigation
heirloom systems of runners climb rows string poles and scaffold

American Fork & Hoe trenching shovel
black wheelbarrow True Temper

hauling wood chips is nice
and after

as if we will last these latest next crises
we resplendent sympathetic

confident lungs wail the grief

pulse a leaf of sky green

never to be seen – it moves somehow
                    is it the sky or is it the planet

sown berm a surge of dirt is land is soil
is a great teacher in the fray

a surface-deep practice of harrowing matters

happenings are a place, the where is inevitable material
a practical claim required for associative

rain or shine

all discourse is "placed,"
*and the heart has its reasons**

close smiles soften together
undemand and sturdy

just passed, just buried
burning anew

         visiting, fresh and bright as I was dreamed

---

*   Stuart Hall, "Cultural Identity and Diaspora" (1990), in *Identity: Community, Culture,*
    Difference, 222.

wells kept in wells, liberation to lifers, burst of cells bust of lings
tamp the surface, tender

watery gnarls irrigation systems find the roots
as they've found us, with our fistfuls of vegetable shapes caked in dirt

for a tired body can sleep
my nail grit, fingertip relief against tomato blood lost blooms

for days the endorphins are a cloudy crimson
a three-pepper hot sauce in a citrus brine

in the cupboard
smoked peppers from last fall infuse with a snip of lilac on the counter

my home and its kitchen are close
almost summer our great hearts I open onto every day we open

WORKS CITED

Bristow, Peggy. "'Whatever You Raise in the Ground You Can Sell It in Chatham': Black Women in Buxton and Chatham, 1850–65." In *"We're Rooted Here and They Can't Pull Us Up": Essays in African Canadian Women's History*, edited by Peggy Bristow with Dionne Brand, Linda Carty, Afua P. Cooper, Sylvia Hamilton, and Adrienne Shadd, 69–140. Toronto: University of Toronto Press, 1994.

Carver, George W. *How to Build Up and Maintain the Virgin Fertility of Our Soils*. Agricultural Research and Experiment Station Bulletin no. 42, Tuskegee Normal and Industrial Institute. Tuskegee, AL: Tuskegee Institute, 1936. www.nal.usda.gov/exhibits/ipd/carver/exhibits/show /bulletins/item/38.

Douglass, Frederick. "First of August Celebration at Dawn Settlement, Canada West – Public Meeting at Chatham – Visit to the Elgin Settlement at Buxton." *Frederick Douglass' Paper*, August 11, 1854. www.loc.gov /item/sn84026366/1854-08-11/ed-1/.

Foden, Jennifer. "What Is Food Insecurity? FoodShare's Paul Taylor Explains (Plus What Canadians Can Do about It)." Food Network, June 25, 2020. www.foodnetwork.ca/article/what-is-food-insecurity/.

Hall, Stuart. "Cultural Identity and Diaspora" (1990). In *Identity: Community, Culture, Difference*, edited by Jonathan Rutherford, 222–237. London: Lawrence & Wishart, 1998.

Hill, Daniel G. *The Freedom-Seekers: Blacks in Early Canada*. Toronto: Stoddart, [1981] 1996.

Hughes, Langston. "Earth Song" (1925). In *Black Nature: Four Centuries of African American Nature Poetry*, edited by Camille T. Dungy, 342. Athens, GA: University of Georgia Press, 2009.

Kroetsch, Robert. *Seed Catalogue*. Winnipeg: Turnstone Press, [1977] 1986.

la paperson [K. Wayne Yang]. *A Third University Is Possible*. Forerunners: Ideas First series. Minneapolis: University of Minnesota Press, 2017. doi. org/10.5749/9781452958460.

Mochama, Vicky. "Black Communities Have Known about Mutual Aid All Along." *Walrus*, September 1, 2020. Updated January 30, 2022. thewalrus .ca/black-communities-have-known-about-mutual-aid-all-along/.

Nicholson, Cecily. ~~a voice that will~~ *clamour* [: *correspondences 1–4*]. Presented as part of *The Pandemic Is a Portal*. SFU Galleries, June 22 to July 31, 2020. www.sfu.ca/galleries/audain-gallery/past1/ThePandemicisaPortal /Nicholson.html.

Nicholson, Cecily, and Mercedes Eng. "Restorative Practices." *BlackFlash* 38, no. 2 (Fall 2021). Issue "A Temporary, Collectively-Held Space," guest-edited by Carmen Papalia. blackflash.ca/2021/10/22/restorative -practices/.

Shadd, Mary A. *A Plea for Emigration, or Notes of Canada West, in Its Moral, Social, and Political Aspect: With Suggestions respecting Mexico, W. Indies and Vancouver's Island, for the Information of Colored Emigrants.* Detroit: n.p. [G.W. Pattison], 1852. www.canadiana.ca/view/oocihm.47542.

Shepard, Marshall. "Frozen Dew, Frost, and Freezes – Do You Know the Difference?" *Forbes*, November 3, 2019. www.forbes.com/sites /marshallshepherd/2019/11/03/frozen-dew-frost-and-freezesdo-you -know-the-difference/?sh=4ce9af7c7232.

Soul Fire Farm. "Each One, Teach One." Accessed June 2022. www .soulfirefarm.org.

Toronto Black Farmers. "About Us." Accessed June 2022. www .torontoblackfarmers.ca/about-us.

Wheatley, Phillis. *The Collected Works of Phillis Wheatley*. Edited by John C. Shields. Schomburg Library of Nineteenth-Century Black Women Writers series. Oxford: Oxford University Press, 1988.

ACKNOWLEDGMENTS

Parts of this book initially formed as commissions for the following: SFU Galleries' *The Pandemic Is a Portal* exhibition; the *Thresholds* digital project hosted by York University; *BlackFlash*, issue 38, no. 2, "A Temporary, Collectively-Held Space," guest-edited by Carmen Papalia, in collaboration with Mercedes Eng; University of Toronto Mississauga's Blackwood Gallery and Ellyn Walker for the *Society for the Diffusion of Useful Knowledge*, issue 12, "BONDING"; and C.S. Giscombe, the Holloway Poetry Series, and the Mixed Blood Project at University of California, Berkeley.

Towards my subsistence during this project, I recognize the support of a Canada Council for the Arts project grant for Literature.

Thank you to the team at Talonbooks for your patience, for holding space, and working hard to bring books to life. A particular thanks to Charles Simard and Catriona Strang for your editorial insight and to Steve Collis for being a great reader, friend, and fellow walker.

The cover for this book forms on a detail from Jan Wade's stunning embroidery work *BREATHE* (2021), held in the Permanent Collection of the Vancouver Art Gallery. My gratitude and respect to this important artist.

Thanks to Nina Reid-Maroney, for your immediate and thoughtful recommendations regarding research towards this project; every suggestion was helpful.

Thank you Nyki Kish, for your care and time in helping me think through language and representation.

Love to folks past and present at Emma's Acres, especially to Nyki, Shay, Zach, and Graham, for the welcome, knowledge-sharing, and camaraderie.

As ever, community and friendship persevere, and because of this I have the capacity to write. Dear Hari Alluri, Phanuel Antwi, Suvi Bains, Arlene Bowman, Neil Brooks, Clint Burnham, Leigh Clarke, Junie Désil, Ivan Drury, Mercedes Eng, David Garneau, Dallas Hunt, the Lyons and Kytes, Otoniya Juliane Okot Bitek, Carmen Papalia, M. NourbeSe Philip, Denise Ryner, Anakana Schofield, Jordan Scott, Harsha Walia, and all you all, thank you.

Love to my familiars. Gratitude and peace to my family near and far, old and new.

Love you Jef, decades now, both epic and quick.

Cecily Nicholson is the author of four books and a past recipient of the Dorothy Livesay Poetry Prize and the Governor General's Literary Award for Poetry. She was the Ellen and Warren Tallman Writer-in-Residence at Simon Fraser University and the Writer-in-Residence at the University of Windsor. She teaches at Emily Carr University of Art + Design, and collaborates with community impacted by carcerality and food insecurity.